PeopleTek's
Leadership Journey I

DRIVING RESULTS THROUGH SELF DISCOVERY

MICHAEL W. KUBLIN

authorHOUSE

AuthorHouse™
1663 Liberty Drive
Bloomington, IN 47403
www.authorhouse.com
Phone: 833-262-8899

Published by AuthorHouse 12/15/2022

ISBN: 978-1-6655-7789-2 (sc)
ISBN: 978-1-6655-7790-8 (e)

Library of Congress Control Number: 2022923147

Print information available on the last page.

Any people depicted in stock imagery provided by Getty Images are models,
and such images are being used for illustrative purposes only.
Certain stock imagery © Getty Images.

This book is printed on acid-free paper.

Dedicated to my Mom, Carol Kublin, for giving me the enthusiasm and interpersonal skills to live my life with meaning and purpose.

CONTENTS

From The Author.. ix

Session 1 Introduction...1

Session 2 Magic Dust 9

Session 3 Myers-Briggs Type Indicator (MBTI) 16

Session 4 DiSC...22

Session 5 Vision, Mission, Goals, Measures = Behavior.........................25

Session 6 Conflict Management 39

Session 7 The Strategic Action Plan 42

Session 8 Listening & Communication..45

Session 9 Understanding and Managing Change 51

Session 10 Team Roles and Magic Dust 62

Session 11 Director/VP Case Study Putting It All Together......................64

Session 12 Wrap-up and Graduation...68

Testimonials..75

From The Author

The Leadership Journey® is a powerful 12 session development program that transforms leadership by providing the tools and techniques that enhance levels of effectiveness. It enables you to understand your strengths and preferences, while better understanding the styles of others.

Leaders of all levels will learn the critical components of effective leadership and determine their most important responsibilities and priorities. You will learn to give and receive feedback in an honoring way, understand unique leadership styles through self-assessment instruments, learn how to handle difficult individuals, enhance your communication and change management style, and build stronger relationships. You will also understand the importance of having written vision, mission and goal statements, and understand why 100% of behaviors must support them.

The Leadership Journey attracts leadership participants with differing backgrounds and different professions. These differences add value through rich participant exchanges, and by the sharing of unique experiences and leadership solutions.

I wish you a successful and enlightening Journey!

Sincerely,
Mike

Session 1

Introduction

PeopleTek's *Leadership Journey*™

The Leadership Journey™ is a leadership effectiveness improvement process; this journey requires that you try various processes in order to be effective and authentic in your own way.

You will be guided through a series of self discoveries that hold the secret for improving your leadership behaviors, techniques and processes. And, you will learn tools that you can immediately apply to the work you are doing today.

To help you do that, we will be working together over a period of time so that we may introduce the tools, put them into practice, and then discuss the results you are experiencing. You will become aware of what is happening to you in your career as a leader, what you want to accomplish and what is getting in your way.

We ask you to keep a learning journal, a Leadership Travel Journal, to document your experience. Please take notes on what you are thinking, feeling and doing as this *Journey* is traveled together!

Workshop Goals

What should you expect to get out of PeopleTek's *Leadership Journey*™? What will you know, feel, and be able to do as a result of this training? When it's completed, you will have:

- An awareness of leadership skills, abilities and behaviors that will allow you to be successful.
- Developed skills, abilities and behaviors that will best advance your leadership capabilities.
- Learned new tools and processes that can be used at any time during your leadership career.
- Learned how to effectively deal with others and how to utilize their unique skills and abilities.
- Be clear about your individual leadership essence/vision and how you should begin to carry it out. Utilize the **Leadership Journey™** to lead you to what you ultimately want to create and achieve.
- Understand how leadership tools can help you most.

Workshop Strategies

How will you be able to achieve these goals? You will learn strategies that will enable you to:

- Be clear about your individual leadership essence/vision and how you should begin to carry it out. Utilize the **Leadership Journey** ™ to lead you to what you ultimately want to create and achieve. **This globe tells you where you are going and if you are on the right path.**

- Understand how leadership tools can help you most. You will find these treasures along the way in your Journey.

- Keep a document of where your leadership has been and where it is going so you and others may refer to it. Record it in your Leadership Travel Journal.

- Have a group of leaders to share experiences with, discuss strategy and plan with. You are not alone; others are on the journey with you.

- Improve business results through the development of leadership skills. Collect a suitcase stuffed full of *memories* and mementos on your Journey.

Workshop Benefits

How do these goals benefit you? We believe you will be able to benefit yourself and your organization by learning how to lead others based on your own inspiration, motivation and insights. You will be able to:

- **understand** what it is you want to create and be able to lead others to that destination.
- **improve** team effectiveness.
- **communicate** what it is you wish to achieve and get others to move in that direction.
- **reduce** the risks of the staff not understanding where the organization is going, what they are responsible for, and how they will be measured.
- **improve** the results for manager effectiveness.
- **network** with others who have similar concerns and desire to grow.

The Leadership Journey™; Who Can Go?

Very simply, anyone who wants to improve their leadership skills is welcomed and encouraged to attend. Leaders of all levels, whether you have direct reports or not, may attend. Insights and concerns from various levels of leaders can be shared. The program is defined so that the individual takes personal accountability of their own leadership development.

Journey Departure:

Why is it a *Journey*? Leadership is not an event but a process which takes time, care, and attention. Most leaders think they need to go to one class and they just "get it". This is not the case. Effective leadership develops over time. It requires analysis of what is effective and what is ineffective. Many leaders do not have a personalized plan for development. They learn by experience, education, trial and error, and self analysis. PeopleTek's *Leadership Journey*™ provides leaders with a proactive opportunity to plan a trip according to their needs. Remember, **the journey is a process and takes place over time**.

The *Leadership Journey*™ provides a method to pick and choose what road you, the leader, prefers to take. After you decide on your travel plan, you will make stops at many destinations. At each stop there will be a **leadership treasure**. This will be a **new skill** or **technique** that you will document in your *Leadership Travel Journal*. There will be books to read and homework along the way.

Who Can Go continued...

The following questions will be treasures each leader will discover along the way.

Why am I taking this _Journey?_ This where the individual determines why they are in a leadership position. This is a very critical discovery. It answers many questions as to where they want to go and what is the **highest level of good they want to achieve as a leader. Are they trying to create business results? If so, which ones do they want?**

Where am I going? Many leaders have no established direction for themselves or their staff. Each leader will establish **a vision, a mission, and goals, and learn associated behaviors.** Without these tools an individual or team will not get to where they want to go.

What types of transportation are available? Here the leader will learn and understand **strategy.** What strategies can be used to get the leaders to go from point A to B? This section will help the leaders look at strategies such as out-tasking and programs such as Six Sigma and how they may fit into their travel plans.

Who can go on PeopleTek's _Leadership Journey_™? A graduate of **PeopleTek's _Leadership Journey_™** said it best: _"anyone who deals with people would benefit. Leaders of all levels should attend. Level is irrelevant as the program helps you understand yourself and better understand others"._

Travel Companions: Once a strategy is defined, there will be resources needed to get you there. Leaders are often confused on how to hire. On this journey, skills and techniques will be learned quickly. They will learn and understand why behaviors are so important. They will learn why this treasure needs to link to their vision, mission and goals.

How you like to travel: Each leader is different and must understand their style and the **style** of those they are bringing on the trip. Tools will be introduced to help them understand themselves and their teams better. Examples include: **Myers-Briggs, DISC, Learning To Listen,** and **Conflict Mode (TKI) Instruments.**

Travel Aides: You will create vision, mission, goals, and capture your preferred styles in the "Journey At A Glance" document. You will also create your own leadership development plan as you travel on your Journey.

PeopleTek's _Leadership Journey_™: Along the way we will pick-up travel plans which **coach** & **develop** your **leadership skills.** At the start of the _Leadership Journey_™ you will need to answer the question _"What type of leader do you want to be"?_ This will determine what road you are likely to choose.

How to handle travel delays and detours: On every trip there are changes. The effective leader must know how to **manage and handle change.**

Why Are We Here?

What things do you as a leader like about your job? What parts don't you like? **New techniques will be learned to create a more enjoyable job.**

You will be answering some questions throughout the *Leadership Journey*™**. Start your** *Leadership Travel Journal* **by answering the following questions:**

> ➤ What are you currently struggling with? What is it that you as a leader are facing that is causing you concern? How can the *Leadership Journey*™ help?

> ➤ What are your dream leadership results? What would the results look like if you were the best leader in the world? What is the highest level of good you want to achieve?

> ➤ What does an effective leader look like, speak like, and act like?

> ➤ Why is a **vision** so important to the leader? What is your **vision**?

> ➤ What is a **mission** and why is that important to the **Leadership** *Journey*™?

> ➤ Why are **goals** so important? What are your **goals**?

> ➤ What **strategies** will you use to carry out your **goals**? Why is **strategy** important?

> ➤ Why are the **resources** you take on the *Leadership Journey*™ so important? Can everyone go on the *Journey*? Why or why not?

> ➤ How will you know you're going in the right direction? How will you know if you are enjoying your *Journey*?

> ➤ What is **leadership style** and why is it important?

> ➤ How do effective leaders handle **change**?

> ➤ How does an effective leader **manage a team**?

> ➤ What is **feedback**, how do you give and receive it, and what do you do when it comes in?

> ➤ Where do the **customers** fit in? Why is that so important?

> ➤ How do you **coach and develop others**?

Definition of Leadership: Leadership is the ability to influence a group to achieve specific goals. The PeopleTek definition is: *"Taking leaders where they've never gone before and would not go by themselves"*.

Managers are people who do things right; leaders are people who do the right thing. **(Warren Bennis)**

There are four major components to being an effective leader:

1. Leaders **captivate** the attention of people through a compelling vision that brings others to a place they have never been before.
2. Leaders make dreams apparent to others and align people with them by **communicating their vision.**
3. Leaders **manage trust and constancy** so that **others will follow them.**
4. Leaders **manage themselves** through clear understanding and effective deployment of their skills.

__Leadership Effectiveness:__ The effectiveness of the leader is based on the attitude of the followers toward the leader. The leader contributes to the quality of the group processes as perceived by followers or other observers. Leadership effectiveness enhances job satisfaction and can influence job performance. (Yukl, 1998).

TOOL RESULTS or a new AWARENESS

PERSONAL ACCOUNTABILITY:

Awareness: What were your insights?

Future Actions: What behaviors do I need to change to really hold myself accountable as a leader?

THE JOHARI WINDOW

This Disclosure/Feedback model of awareness known as the Johari Window is named after Joseph Luft and Harry Ingham. It was first used in an information session at the Western Training Laboratory in Group Development in 1955.

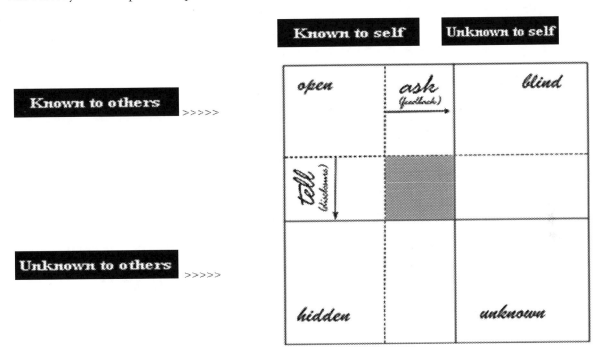

The four panes of the window represent the following:

- O_ _ _: The open area is that part of our conscious self - our attitudes, behavior, motivation, values, way of life - of which **we are aware** and which is **known to others.** We move within this area with freedom. We are "open books".

- H_ _ _ _ _: Our hidden area **cannot be known to others unless we disclose it**. There is that which we freely keep within ourselves, and that which we retain out of fear. The degree to which we share ourselves with others (disclosure) is the degree to which we can be known.

- B_ _ _ _ :There are **things about ourselves which we do not know**, but that others can see more clearly; or things we imagine to be true of ourselves for a variety of reasons but that others do not see at all. When others say what they see (feedback), in a supportive, responsible way, and we are able to hear it; in that way we are able to test the reality of who we are and are able to grow.

- U_ _ _ _ _ _: We are more rich and complex than that which we and others know, but from time to time something happens - is felt, read, heard, dreamed - something from our unconscious is revealed. Then we "know" what we have never "known" before.

- It is through disclosure and feedback that our open pane is expanded and that we gain access to the potential within us represented by the unknown pane.

Ice Breaker- Am I A Rare Find?

Answer any of the five questions below.

1. I am the _____ (1ˢᵗ, middle, youngest) sibling in my family.

2. To pass time I like to _____.

3. I think most people are _____.

4. Other people describe me as _____ and _____.

5. Our world would be a better place if only people would?

6. I work because _____.

7. A true friend is _____ and _____.

8. My second career choice would be _____.

9. I wish I could change _____.

10. When I'm not at work, I like to _____.

SESSION 2

Magic Dust

Objective

In **Session 2** of **PeopleTek's** *Leadership Journey*®, we will **examine our uniqueness**, our **special skills and our strengths as a leader**. We will also review the special skills and strengths of others. Most often we scrutinize what we are not good at. During the *Leadership Journey* ® we will analyze what we are good at; what are our unique skills and abilities as a leader? How do we market them? How do we communicate them to others? Who are we offering those services to and how much value do we place on them?

We will also evaluate some popular and well-known public leaders to understand what makes them so effective. Why did they choose this position, what is their highest hope of accomplishment, how do they feel they are progressing, what have they been experiencing, what type of help do they need? We will understand the concept of *Magic Dust* and how it applies to us and others.

We will understand the difference between **Leadership**, **Management**, **Coaching** and **Technician** and determine for ourselves where we spend most of our time. We will measure our effectiveness as leaders and determine what courses of action we need to take to become better leaders.

Finally, we will discuss **giving and receiving feedback** in an honoring way.

Effective Leadership Traits

Look back on the leadership traits that you identified as being important to you in session 1. There is no one absolute list of traits that will make you successful but here are some that are essential to finding your leadership essence or *Magic Dust*.

➤ True leaders lead integrated lives in which their careers and their personal lives fit seamlessly and harmoniously together.

➤ Their ambition, talent and capacity to learn have served them rather than enslaved them.

➤ These leaders have identified their true calling and fulfilled their own genius through passion, energy and focus.

➤ As the leader learned to fulfill his/her own vision, they also learned to assist employees to fulfill their own visions.

➤ True leaders are persistent and don't give up easily.

EXERCISE 2.1 — The Leadership Travel Profile:

It's important to assess our styles, behaviors, and skills and develop a profile of ourselves. We may be challenged to do so, but there's a need to uncover the essence of who we truly are.

SELF ASSESSMENT
Answer the following questions using a rating scale of 1-8

1 = no
2 or 3 = infrequently
4 = sometimes
5 or 6 = frequently
7 = almost always
8 = always

1. I have thought about what it is I want to do and accomplish in my life.   1 2 3 4 5 6 7 8

2. I understand what a SMART goal is.   1 2 3 4 5 6 7 8

3. I understand others have unique strengths and talents.   1 2 3 4 5 6 7 8

4. I know that communication and feedback are key tools for leaders.   1 2 3 4 5 6 7 8

5. I am comfortable with conflict and don't avoid it.   1 2 3 4 5 6 7 8

6. I understand the value of coaching and development   1 2 3 4 5 6 7 8

7. I understand the value of taking a chance.   1 2 3 4 5 6 7 8

8. I am regularly taking steps in the direction of my life plan.   1 2 3 4 5 6 7 8

9. My goals are documented. I review them and take action regularly.   1 2 3 4 5 6 7 8

10. I take specific steps to delegate assignments based on the strengths and talents of others.   1 2 3 4 5 6 7 8

11. I regularly conduct one on one meetings with my team and others.   1 2 3 4 5 6 7 8

12. I utilize my conflict skills effectively when approaching difficult situations   1 2 3 4 5 6 7 8

13. I utilize my coaching and mentoring in my staff & customer interactions.   1 2 3 4 5 6 7 8

14. I fail and I succeed and debrief both with my staff.   1 2 3 4 5 6 7 8

EXERCISE 2.2 — The Leadership Travel Journal

THE LEADERSHIP TRAVEL JOURNAL

Date:

a) What made me choose a leadership position?

b) What do I feel is needed for me to be a more successful leader?

c) What special leadership qualities do I bring to this or any organization?

d) What makes a great leader? Who are some of the past leaders that have inspired me? Could they be leaders in your life? What attributes did they have?

e) I was most inspired in school by…

f) I was most inspired in a job by…

g) The most valuable things I learned in any job have been…

EXERCISE 2.2 — The Leadership Travel Journal, continued...

The Leadership Travel Journal

Date:

h)   What is the highest level of good I want to achieve?

i)   What are some lessons learned from past experiences that I would like to impart to others?

j)   How have any of my previous jobs made an impact on my life and what would I like others to learn about?

k)   What are some things I would like to change?

l)   What are some of the travel delays, detours, and roadblocks I am facing now?

m)   What do I need now in order to have a successful *Leadership Journey®*?

n)   What I still want to learn about leadership is...

Key Definitions to Understand and Talk About in the *Leadership Journey*®:

➤ **LEADERSHIP**:   Taking others where they have not been before and would not go by themselves.

➤ **MANAGEMENT**:   Planning, Organizing, Controlling, and Following-up.

➤ **COACHING**:   Helping others achieve their desired goals and objectives.

➤ **TECHNICIAN**:   Doing the job or task extremely well.

Managing vs. Leading

• Concerned with task	• The BIG picture
• Short range view	• Long range view
• Needs rules	• Needs risks
• Rigid structure	• Flexible structure
• Fears mistakes	• Welcomes mistakes
• Stable environment	• Dynamic environment
• Relies on controls	• Inspires trust
• The bottom line	• Sees the horizon
• Is reactive	• Is proactive
• Does things right	• Does the right thing

Introduction to Feedback

The 360 Feedback Process

Purpose: To help you clarify your Magic Dust and 'open' any blind spots in your leadership behaviors.

Based on your 360 Feedback and other learnings from your Leadership Journey we will help you create your VMGM=B document or an Individual Development Plan (IDP). This process is a critical component of your Journey

Steps in the Process:

1. Create a list of the people you want to ask to provide feedback and review with your leader. These are your 'raters'. Please include:

   - your leader(s) – This is the person(s) to whom you directly report.
   - all of your immediate peers - those who report to your leader with you
   - all of your direct reports – those who report to you
   - other peers, customers, etc. with whom you have a lot of contact
   - do not limit the feedback to your "fans".
   - include a minimum of 12-15 raters - no maximum; however, only include those with sufficient recent contact to provide a meaningful, current view of your leadership.

   Note: There must be a minimum of 2 per category other than leader, so for example if you only have 1 direct report, you can include them in misc. This is important to maintain the anonymity of the process. Again, with the exception of your leader, a minimum of 2 per category are required.

2. You will receive instructions to enter your rater data into a spreadsheet. Please return as directed, by the deadline set by your Coach/Facilitator.
3. As soon as you complete your list, send your raters a letter letting them know that you are requesting their feedback and ask them for their support. (A sample will be provided with your spreadsheet instructions.)
4. When we have your spreadsheet we will send you and your raters a link for the 360 feedback tool.
5. You and your raters will be requested to complete by a specific date.
6. One-on-one telephone coaching feedback sessions will be scheduled for each Journey participant with your Executive Coach/Facilitator
7. Everyone will be asked to share their strengths and what they are working on with your Leadership Journey class.
8. You are encouraged to communicate with everyone you asked to rate you to express your appreciation for their time and to share with them what they said were your strengths and what, based on your feedback, you will be working on improving. Often what you will choose to work on is to stop over-using one of your strengths!

Myers-Briggs Type Indicator (MBTI)

Objective

In Session 3 of PeopleTek's *Leadership Journey®* we will concentrate on understanding our behavior and leadership traits as well as those we are leading. The MYERS-BRIGGS Type Indicator (MBTI) is the first of several instruments that we will be using, and the results will improve our ability to understand:

➢ our unique strengths
➢ the unique strengths of others
➢ understand the concept of over-using a skill or strength and under-using a skill or strength
➢ begin process of giving and receiving feedback in a healthy, honoring manner

The instruments will provide us feedback on our style of communication, how we prefer to lead others, make decisions, approach change and many others.

We as leaders become stronger as we increase our understanding of ourselves and others. With this knowledge, we will be able to develop strategies to motivate and inspire our teams to achieve the results we desire. We will learn and utilize new tools to help us with what behaviors are bringing us closer to our vision, and which ones are interfering with our success.

TOOLS

The tools used in the next few sessions are **Myers-Briggs (MBTI), DiSC, Leadership, 6 Types Of Genius, and Learning To Listen.** For this session, we will focus on the **Myers-Briggs (MBTI)** instrument and how it can assist us with our leadership skills and abilities. (We will address the other instruments in detail in upcoming sessions.) The **Myers-Briggs** is the first instrument used that will enlighten us to our leadership skills and abilities. These characteristics are linked to our uniqueness as individuals and leaders. Understanding the way we lead others and what we prefer as leaders can help us determine effective approaches to managing, motivating and inspiring others in their positions to accomplish their organizational goals.

We will also provide techniques that will enable you as leaders to identify, understand and eliminate the road blocks to effectively communicating with your team. Finally, we will look at the concept of change from the leader's perspective; how are people affected by change and what things to look for.

Continue to **use your** *Leadership Travel Journal* to record your thoughts as you develop your understanding of the information. Be sure to record those specific techniques that really resonate and make sense to you and your specific leadership style.

As with all powerful processes there is a key or symbol that helps us learn how it works.

Each of the following dichotomies are associated with a unique key or symbol

Battery	**Where do we get our energy from and where do we like to focus our attention?** **Extraversion (E) Introversion (I)**
Satellite	**How do we take in information?** **Sensing (S) iNtuition (N)**
Jury Box	**How do we finally make our decision once our information is in?** **Thinking (T) or Feeling (F)**
Tug of War	**How do we like to live in this world?** **Judging (J) or Perceiving (P)**

MYERS-BRIGGS Type Indicator (MBTI) Insights

1. Where do we get our energy from? Extraverts (E) Introverts (I)

As with all powerful processes there is a **key or symbol** that helps us learn how it works. Each of the following preferences are associated with a unique **key or symbol.**

BATTERY- Where we get our E _ _ _ _ _ from.

The E's prefer P _ _ _ _ _, P _ _ _ _ _, and T _ _ _ _ _.

The I's prefer I _ _ _ _ and C _ _ _ _ _ _ _.

Name some words that come to your mind that describes someone who gets their <u>energy</u> from <u>People, Places and Things</u>:

What if we over use this trait what words might be your perception?

Name some words that come to your mind that describes someone who gets their energy from <u>Ideas and Concepts</u>:

What if we over use this trait what words might be your perception?

I ask three questions: (These same questions will be used for all type indicators)

1. Have you ever seen this behavior on your teams? (positive or negative)
2. Have you ever seen this behavior impact business results? (positive or negative)
   Give specific examples:

3. Do we tend to talk about it with the person in a healthy, honoring, respectful, nurturing way?

2. How do we prefer to take in our information: Sensors (S) Intuitives (N)

Satellite Dish- How we prefer to take in our I _ _ _ _ _ _ _ _ _ _. Do we take our <u>information</u> in based on details and facts or our gut or sixth sense?.

The S's prefer D _ _ _ _ _ _ and F _ _ _ _.

The N's prefer using their G _ _ .

The '**Sensors**' (**S**) want to know who, what, when, where, why and how many.

The '**Intuitives**' (**N**) want to go beyond details and facts and use what they think based on their intuition or 6th sense.

Name some words that come to your mind that describes someone who prefers to take their information in based on <u>details and facts</u>:

What if we over use this trait what words might be your perception?

Name some words that come to your mind that describes someone who prefers to take their information in based on their "gut or 6th sense":

What if we over use this trait what words might be your perception?

3. How do we finally decide once our information is in:
'Thinkers' (T) or 'Feelers' (F)

JURY BOX:
Do we decide based on L _ _ _ _ and F _ _ _ _ .?

Do we decide based on how other's F _ _ _ about the decision?

The T's base their decision on logic and facts

The F's base their decision on how others will feel about it

Name some words that come to your mind that describes someone who prefers to make their decisions based on <u>logic and facts</u>?

What if we overuse this trait what words might come to mind?

Name some words that come to your mind that describes someone who prefers to make their decisions based on how others will <u>feel</u> about the decision?

What if we overuse this trait what words might come to mind?

4. How do we like to live in this world?
'Judgment' (J) or 'Perception' (P)

TUG of WAR:

The J's like to live in a world that is very P _ _ _ _ _ _ and O _ _ _ _ _ _ .

The P's like to live in a world that is very F _ _ _ _ _ _ _ and S _ _ _ _ _ _ _ _ _ _ .

Name some words that come to your mind that describes someone who prefers to live in a world that is very <u>planned and orderly</u>:

What if we overuse this trait what words might come to mind?

Name some words that come to your mind that describes someone who prefers to live in a world that is <u>flexible and spontaneous</u>:

What if we overuse this trait what words might come to mind?

WHAT IS YOUR BEST FIT MYERS-BRIGGS TYPE?

_____

EXERCISE 3.1 – Myers-Briggs (MBTI) Type Indicator

Review what you have learned about yourself from the **MBTI** instrument:

1. Are you **overusing** any of your **skills and abilities**?

2. Are you **under-using** any of your **skills and abilities**?

3. Did you experience any **"a-ha's"** about your **essence**?

4. Did you experience any **insights** about your **staff**?

5. **Jot down key points** you have learned through this exercise in your **Leadership Travel Journal**.

6. What is your **MBTI Type**?

Encouraging Feedback: Steps in The Process

1. **ASK**: Ask your co-workers for feedback. The simple act of asking sends a message that you value their opinion and that you, would consider changing based upon their input.

2. **LISTEN**: Listen to what they say. Try not to evaluate whether they are "right" or wrong," simply accept their opinions as *their* perceptions of reality. Avoid trying to defend your actions.

3. **THINK**: Think about their input before reacting. Make sure you avoid overreacting or making commitments that you may not be willing or able to keep in the future. *Under-commit* and *over-deliver.*

4. **THANK**: Express your appreciation for the feedback. Letting *you* know what they think in an act that may require courage. Take the time to personally say "thank-you."

5. **RESPOND**: Respond to the people who gave you feedback. After careful thought, let them know the 1–3 areas where you plan to change. Keep it simple; do not try to change too many behaviors.

6. **INVOLVE**: Involve them in the change process. Ask them if they have any further suggestions. *Recruit them* to help you as you try to change. Ask for their ongoing support.

7. **CHANGE**: Do something about the feedback. Write down your 1–3 areas for change and keep these in front of you. Remind yourself to give these 1–3 areas the priority they deserve. Monitor your own behavior on a timely basis.

8. **FOLLOW-UP**: Follow up with your co-workers approximately every 3-4 months. Ask them if *they* think that you are changing. When they start to say you have changed, they begin to *believe* that you have changed.

SESSION 4

DiSC

Objective

In **Session 4** of **PeopleTek's** *Leadership Journey®* we will become familiar with our DiSC instrument results. This is the second tool for the program. This tool will help you further uncover and understand your unique skills and abilities, your Magic Dust.

The **DiSC** will enable you as a leader 1) determine your approach to an assignment or task, 2) what is important to you, 3) how it would be perceived by others and 4) what may be your motivation or desire as you behave. This information is crucial to us as leaders since we act based on what we are thinking. Too many of us do not slow down enough to permit reflection on how our actions are impacting ourselves and others.

Results of the **DiSC** instrument in this session of the *Leadership Journey®* gives us a chance to receive feedback about how we approach our tasks, assignments and leadership challenges. Understanding this information will enable us to determine if we are taking the appropriate approach for handling certain tasks and leadership challenges. What we learned as young adults or in other situations may not be effective for us today.

We can understand the unique style and strengths of our colleagues and staff members. We can instruct our staff on what we want from them and how they can expect us to behave. They can then better understand how to approach us, what is important to us and how it can help us be more successful as leaders. This information will help us build stronger relationships with our staff and enable us to motivate and inspire others based on their individual preferences, not ours.

Note: *In this session we will review DiSC Workplace*

EXERCISE 4.1 — DiSC Tool Results

Review what you have learned about yourself from the **DiSC** instrument:

1. Are you **over-using** any of your **skills and abilities**?

2. Are you **under-using** any of your **skills and abilities**?

3. Did you experience any **"a-ha's"** about your **essence**?

4. Did you experience any **insights** about your **staff**?

5. **Jot down key points** you have learned through this exercise in your **Leadership Travel Journal**.

6. What is your **DiSC predominant style**? Does it help you identify your **Magic Dust**?

DiSC: Summary of Preferences

Style	D	i	S	C
Basic Tendencies	Fast Paced Task-oriented	Fast Paced People-oriented	Slow Paced People-oriented	Slow Paced Task-oriented
Greatest Strengths	Decisive Action Takes Charge Gets Results Self-Confident Independent Risk-Taker	Fun-Loving Involved Enthusiastic Emotional Optimistic Good Communicator	Patient Easy Going Team Player Calming Influence Stability Systematic	Accurate Analytical Detailed High Standards Intuitive Controlled
Natural Limitations	Impatient Stubborn Blunt	Disorganized Not Detail-Oriented Unrealistic	Indecisive Over-Accommodating Too Passive	Too Critical Perfectionist Overly Sensitive
Communication	One Way Direct "Bottom Line"	Positive Inspiring Persuasive	Two way Best Listener Empathetic Feedback	Diplomatic Good Listener Provides Details
Fears	Being Taken Advantage Of	Loss of Social Approval	Loss of Stability	Criticism of Their Work or Performance
Under Pressure	Autocratic Aggressive Demanding	Attacks (But May Avoid Public Confrontation)	Acquiesces Tolerates Complies	Avoids Ignores Plans Strategy
Money Viewed As A Means Of	Power	Freedom	Showing Love	Insuring Security
Decision Making	Quick: Result-Focused Very Few Facts	Impulsive Whether It "Feels" Right	Relational Trust In Others	Reluctant Needs A lot Of Information
Greatest Needs	Challenges Change Choices Direct Answers	Fun Activities Social Recognition Freedom From Details	Status Quo/ Security Time to Adjust to Change, Conflict Free Environment	Time to Do Quality Work Personal Support No Surprises
Recovery	Physical Activity	Social Time	Nothing Time	Private

Vision, Mission, Goals, Measures = Behavior

As with all powerful processes there is a key or symbol that helps us learn how it works. With this leadership process there are four symbols.

	V _____
	M _____
	G _____
	M _____

V M G M = B

VISION =

It's a <u>DREAM</u> or <u>ASPIRATION</u> that you as the leader have for yourself and your organization. The vision provides <u>DIRECTION</u> and guides us to a place far away. It may be unattainable but we can try and focus our attention and make strides for getting there.

MISSION=

Represents <u>WHAT</u> you are going to do and <u>HOW</u> you're going to do it to carry out the vision. It makes the vision come closer to us; it brings the vision alive for us and makes it more personal. The mission begins to bring <u>CLARITY</u> to our vision.

GOALS=

Bring 100 percent personal clarity to your vision and mission. It requires <u>ACTION</u>. Think in terms of <u>WHAT, WHEN, and HOW</u>, the actions will be carried out, by whom and <u>WHEN</u>.

The goals must be "SMART":
Specific Measurable Actionable/Achievable Realistic Timebound

METRICS or TAPE MEASURE=

Symbolizes measurement and provides guidance and direction. It also acts as a compass letting us know if we are not on track and if our direction or behavior requires change.

<u>VISION, MISSION, GOALS, and MEASURES</u> dictate <u>ALL</u> of our leadership, team and organizational <u>behaviors</u>. By creating it on purpose, rather than by chance or mistake, we will be more successful organizations and deliver better results for our customers, shareholders and ourselves.

Complete the following exercise on developing vision, mission and goals for an organization.

EXERCISE 5.1 — Vision, Mission and Goals Preparation and Planning

1. What services do we or should we offer? What differentiates us from our competition?

2. Who is or could be our customer? Describe an ideal customer.

3. From our customer's viewpoint, what does our customer want?

4. Why will the customers buy this product or service? What value does this service provide the customer? What unique benefits does this service provide the customer?

5. What passion(s) are you trying to satisfy by building this business? What beliefs do you have that will impact this business? What is the highest good this business can achieve? Who will benefit from this business?

6. Are we customer focused, operations focused or product focused? If so, what behaviors should we use, and why should we use them, with each other to be successful?

7. Think about a time when you were really excited about what was happening at work. Describe what was happening. What was exciting about it, and what made it so important?

8. Generalize from that experience to answer the following questions:

   a) What's really exciting and important about the work I do?

   b) What do I really value about the work I do?

Spend a few moments reflecting on the most important values of our organization – not necessarily the values that are currently operating but the answers to these questions.

9. What values do we want to live by? What values do we want to be known for?

10. What accomplishments would you like to celebrate this year? Next year? What targets will you aim for? Examples: Financial, Marketing and Sales, Operations, Human Resources, Engineering, R&D, others.

Creating Your Mission Statement

The mission statement describes the **purpose** for which your product, service or work unit exists. It always answers the question "Why will customers buy or use this product or service"? Your **mission statement should cover** the following:

- Your commitments and promises
- A balance of business needs with customer needs
- Reflection of your passion and commitment

Drawing Forth a Personal Vision

Having a **vision** is not limited to the business world. The following exercise is intended to help you **define your personal vision** – what you want to create of yourself and the world around you.

EXERCISE 5.2 – Creating Your Personal Vision

To prepare:

Pick a place that you can sit or recline in privacy, a quiet and relaxed space to write, with comfortable furniture and no visual distractions. Play a favorite piece of music if you like. Give yourself a block of time without visitors, phone calls or hassles...no interruptions.

Step 1

Bring yourself to a reflective state of mind. Take a few deep breaths, let go of any tension as you exhale.

Recall an image or memory that is meaningful to you. It could be a favorite spot in nature, an encounter with a person, an image of an animal, a memory of a significant event. Shut your eyes for a moment and stay with that image. Put yourself into that moment by feeling, touching, experiencing, tasting what is going on. Open your eyes and answer the following questions.

Imagine achieving a result in your life that you deeply desire – you live where you want to live, you do the work you want to do, you have the relationships you want to have. Ignore how possible or impossible it seems. **Write down** or sketch the experience you have imagined, using the present tense, as if it is happening now.

- What does it look like?
- What does it feel like?
- What words would you use to describe it?

EXERCISE 5.2 – Creating Your Personal Vision, continued...

<u>Step 2</u>

Reflect on your first vision. Is this vision close to what you actually want? Consider some of the reasons you may find articulating a vision difficult. If any of these fit you, take time to work through the issue.

- I can't have what I want. Are child hood habits of fear of failure getting in the way? Suspend your doubts, worries and fears. Write as if anything is possible.
- I want what someone else wants. Are you choosing a vision based on what someone else – a parent, spouse, supervisor – wants for you? For now concentrate only on what you want.
- It doesn't matter what I want. Are you assuming that what you want is not important? Just get any old thing down on paper? For now assume that you do deserve the rewards you desire.
- I am afraid of what I want. Are you afraid that wanting things will get out of control? What if you don't want your job anymore? This is 'your' vision so you can set your own limits. If a subject frightens you, you can decide to stay away from it.
- I don't know what I want. Everyone has a vision within them. Inability to create a vision is a measure of despair. If you have hope, you have a vision.
- I know what I want, but I can't have it at work. Do you fear that your personal vision will not be compatible with your organization's attitude? Check it out with other people. If it really doesn't fit this organization, your vision may be to find some other place to work.

<u>Step 3</u>

Describe your personal vision by answering the following questions. Write in the present tense and adjust the categories to fit your needs. This should give you a more complete picture of your vision.

Imagine achieving the results in your life that you deeply desire. What would they look like? What would they feel like? What words would you use to describe them?

Self-image: If you could be the kind of person you wanted what would your qualities be?

Tangibles: What material things would you like to own?

Home: What is your ideal living environment?

Health: What is your desire for health, fitness, athletics and anything to do with your body?

EXERCISE 5.2 – Creating Your Personal Vision, continued...

Relationships: What type of relationships would you like to have with friends, family, co-workers and others?

Work: What is your ideal professional or vocational situation? What impact would you like your efforts to have?

Personal pursuits: What would you like to create in the arena of individual learning, travel, reading and other activities?

Community: What is your vision for the community or society you live in?
Other: What else, in any other arena of your life, would you like to create?
Life purpose: Imagine that your life has a unique purpose – fulfilled through what you do, your interrelationships, and the way you live. Describe that purpose.

Step 4

Expand and clarify your vision. Like most people, likely you will have a combination of selfless and self-centered elements. To clarify your vision, go through your list and ask yourself:

o   If I could have it now, would I take it?
o   If I have it now, what does that bring me?

Source: Senge, P. (1994). The Fifth Discipline Fieldbook. Doubleday.

You are now ready to create your personal vision statement. **Use the space provided to define your personal vision statement.**

My Personal Vision Statement is:

VMGM=B Presentation

We know that if we carefully think through our Vision, Mission, Goals and Measures it will drive our own behaviors, as well as the behaviors of our organization. As you prepare your presentation to share with your leader and your Journey classmates, also document the behaviors that will have to shift to accomplish your Vision, Mission and Goals (for you and/or your organization.)

Vision, Mission, Goals, Measures = Behaviors

My Vision is:

My Missions is:

GOAL	MEASURE
Goal 1 description (one or two sentences or phrases)	**Measure one due date: mm/dd/yy** **Measure two due date: mm/dd/yy**
Goal 2 description (one or two sentences or phrases)	**Measure one due date: mm/dd/yy** **Measure two due date: mm/dd/yy**
Goal 3 description (one or two sentences or phrases)	**Measure one due date: mm/dd/yy** **Measure two due date: mm/dd/yy**
Goal 4 description (one or two sentences or phrases)	**Measure one due date: mm/dd/yy** **Measure two due date: mm/dd/yy**

EXERCISE 5.3 — Business On Paper EXERCISE

EXERCISE A - Rancho Lujoso Spa and Resort

You recently were hired to manage a new health and fitness spa called "Rancho Lujoso Spa and Resort". The company specializes in health and fitness for the few who want a special private place to go and get into shape and relax.

They feature a small exercise facility that has all the appropriate equipment for your total care. Each piece of equipment overlooks the mountains. They specialize in making you feel like you are one-in-a-million. They do this by having scented candles, clean pressed towels, soft music, and employees that know you by name.

They offer a small locker room that features private showers, a steam room, sauna and whirlpool. They clean the shower after each person leaves. They also offer a quiet room for relaxing that overlooks a waterfall. They offer additional group training, which is included in their fee structure.

Together with the other managers at the spa you have been asked to determine:

1. Is the company **operations excellent, customer intimate or product innovative**? What would be your fee structure? High or low?

2. A company **vision statement**.

3. What **skills and abilities** (both technical and customer service) would you need to hire to support the vision of the spa?

4. What would be **one goal**?

5. What would you base your employee performance appraisal and **reward and recognition program** on?

6. What is one **measure** which could determine if you are succeeding or not?

Exercise 5.3 — Business On Paper Exercise, continued...

Exercise B – Solid Perfect Fitness

You recently were hired to manage a new health and fitness company called "Solid Perfect Fitness".

The company specializes in total fitness for everyone who wants to get into shape. They feature a 50,000 square foot open facility with every possible piece of body building equipment in existence.

They have mirrors located on every wall, play rock and roll and disco music. They offer shower, steam, and sauna facilities. They have low monthly fees and they offer discounts for personal training.

They are open 24 by 7 and have many locations and are aggressive at getting new customers with their marketing strategy.

Together with the other managers at the spa you have been asked to determine:

1. Is the company **operations excellent**, **customer intimate** or **product innovative**? What would be your fee structure? High or low?

2. A company **vision statement**.

3. What **skills and abilities** (both technical and customer service) would you need to hire to support the vision of the spa?

4. What would be one **goal**?

5. What would you base your employee performance appraisal and **reward and recognition program** on?

6. What is one **measure** which could determine if you are succeeding or not?

*"People who write down their objectives achieve most of all.
Here's how."*

GETTING YOUR GOALS Article by Robert McGarvey

It was just a year ago that 36-year-old Jeff Jackson lost his job as sales manager at a Los Angeles car dealership. A search turned up no comparable openings around town, and Jackson didn't relish a return to a dealership's floor as a salesman. "So I made up my mind to do something entirely different-real estate," says Jackson. Not as a Realtor, mind you, but as an investor, despite the fact he's run through the bulk of his savings while unemployed. "That became my goal," he says. "I wanted to own $1 million in investment properties inside a year."

But it didn't take 12 months- just 10 were needed- and today Jackson heads a syndicate that owns a beachfront triplex plus two multiunit apartment complexes in an appreciating area. Says Jackson, "You know what? Even on the worst days a year ago, I knew I'd have what I have today! – I can prove it." With that Jackson pulls out a yellow legal-sized sheet of paper, dated June 30, 1988, and headed "Goals for the year." Everything he has today is itemized on that list.

Some may think that it is just a coincidence that Jackson, mired in a career slump, made a list of what he wanted and now has it. But there's a direct and strong connection between his "want list" and his achievements.

Sift through the reams of information cataloging the difference between high and low performers and two shocking facts emerge: **The people who have goals achieve far more than those who don't,** and **those who have written goals achieve the most of all.** Forrest H. Patton, a motivational speaker and author of *Force of Persuasion*, vividly underlines these facts.

"A study was made of alumni 10 years out of Harvard to find out how many were achieving their goals," explains Patton. "An astounding 83 percent had no goals at all. Fourteen percent had specific goals but they were not written down. Their average earnings were three times what those in the 83 percent group were earning. However, the three percent who had written goals were earning 10 times that of the 83 percent group."

Maxwell Maltz, author of Psycho–Cybernetics and an acclaimed researcher into the functioning of the human brain, insists there is nothing unexpected about these results. According to Maltz, we are functionally akin to bicycles: Unless we're moving forward toward an objective, we will fall- and fail.

And that's exactly what a goal is-an objective. Picture a football game without goals. There would be chaos on the field for a few minutes, and pretty soon everybody would give up and go home because the hubbub would be pointless.

With the goals in place, it's a completely different story. Goals give the players a reason to be there "to compete and to excel".

J.C. Penny, founder of the retail store chain which bears his name, expressed the same thought in more powerful language: "Give me a stock clerk with a goal, and I will give you a man who will make history. Give me a man without a goal, and I will give you a stock clerk."

Understand that a goal is not "I want to be wealthy" or "I want to be famous." Those may be wishes, and they may be strongly held, but they're not goals. Real estate investor Jackson didn't just dream about owning property-knowing the odds were against him, he wrote out "a detailed plan, including what I would buy and how I would finance it," he explains. Specificity, an exactness of detail, is needed to make a goal worth having. "If you find you can't measure it, rate it, or describe it, you probably can forget it as a goal," says Dr. Michael LeBoeuf, author of Working Smart.

"A lack of clarity of intent" is high on the list of causes for failure to achieve goals, adds Dick Sutphen, a seminar leader and author of both videotapes and audiotapes on goals. "If you really want to succeed, be very clear about your intent," stresses Sutphen. "Be absolutely positively 100 percent sure what you want to do and what you seek you accomplish."

But goal identification is not always easy. Think for just an instant, and dozens of goals may pop up in your imagination-to be president of General Motors, a millionaire, happily married, a U.S. Senator, a movie star, and so on. The possibilities are unlimited. But unlimited possibilities can make achievement of any of them of them impossible. A narrowing of focus is the first step toward getting what you want.

"It's easy to dream," observers Barbara Sher, author of Wishcraft. "With just a little encouragement you can close your eyes and conjure up a whole new life for yourself. But if you want to make that life come true, you will have to start by choosing one piece of it and deciding that that's the one you're going to go for first. Then you may still have to do a little work on that piece to turn it into something that's really reachable-not a mirage that keeps receding ahead of you.

Out of all the possibilities, how will you know if you've picked the right goal? Dr. Dru Scott, head of a San Francisco-based management education firm, offers the guideline: "Imagine that you're being interviewed by a newspaper reporter on your hundredth birthday and are asked to name your most important accomplishments. How would you like to answer?'

Or try Sher's prescription: "When you say, 'This is what I want,' you're not fooling. If I could wave a magic wand and, poof, you'd have that goal right now, you honestly think you'd be delighted."

It's at this juncture that more than a few falter, wondering if they picked the wrong goal. Understand, however, that just about any goal is worth having—and worth achieving. And remember that "goals aren't written in blood," as Sher points out.

Just as economic conditions or evolving technology will lead an IBM or Chrysler to revise its goals, so too is flexibility advised for individuals. "As a growing person, your needs and values will be forever evolving," says LeBoeuf. "Consequently, you have to reevaluate and often modify, discard, or replace some of your goals."

If you've set as your goal to be president of your company and second thoughts pop up—it's too much responsibility, or it would take away too much from family and social life—that's no big deal. Nothing's been lost. By working toward the presidency, you've probably made yourself into an extraordinary employee. There have been accomplishments along the way toward that now-discarded goal—and odds are that those accomplishments will dramatically enhance the achievement of new, revised goals.

When defining your goals, LeBoeuf suggests that they be picked for several different time frames, and he provides a three-step process for doing just that. There should be a lifetime goal, which sums up the results you most want to accomplish over the course of your life. Next come intermediate goals—what you wish to accomplish in less than a year. The last step is to list your daily goals—what do you want to do today?

Newcomers to goal-setting frequently admit to feeling overwhelmed when confronting the task of detailing goal for the next half-century. But there is a built-in logic to the method. The lifetime goal functions as the keystone; it's the pivot around which the rest of the goals revolve. The intermediate goals directly feed into it, while the daily goals ideally contribute in a straight-line fashion to both the intermediate and lifetime goals.

Some theorists add in five-year goals as a step between the yearly and the lifetime goals. But motivational speaker Dave Grant proposes that the best strategy for many is to start small. "Start with small goals and gain an experience of accomplishment and success," advises Grant. "Once you learn you can go after something and make it happen, it makes it that much easier to set and achieve bigger and bigger goals."

Remember, however, that achieving any goal is not done by magic. There is work involved. A first step recommended by Grant is to set a target date—when will you achieve the goal?—and to write it and the goal itself down. "Most people fail in their goal-setting because they're just thinking about their goals. They're not committed to them," explains Grant. "Thinking is not a commitment. Writing it down is."

Nobody knows why a written goal is more effective than one that's known and understood but not committed to paper. Some psychologists theorize that writing triggers important processes in the subconscious processes that also get the subconscious working toward the written goals. But other theorists scoff at that. In the hard-boiled and practical world of achievements, the reasons why don't really matter.

The undebatable benefits that come from taking the time to commit goals to paper are what's important.

Every popular method of helping to attain your goals involves about the same commitment, work, and effort.

But while the power of written goals is indisputable, many of us will not commit them to paper. The chief block is fear. We're afraid of taking on a goal because of the consequences of failure. Writing it down makes the goal concrete and undeniable, and that just magnifies the potential for pain if the endeavor fails. "We all have a hard time handling disappointment," says Grant. "How do we avoid it? By not setting any goals. Do that, and you'll never be disappointed. Trouble is you also can be sure you won't accomplish anything."

The antidote? For Dr. Denis Waitley, a leading authority of high performance, it's desire. "Desire sparks activity, which burns up excess adrenaline in the system, keeps the mind busy, and the hope of achievement alive. Inactivity breeds despondency, brings forth dark imaginings, and distorts situations out of all proportion to reality. When fear begins to beg for attention, the winner gets busy and things regain their proper perspective."

A way to get busy, says Grant, is to take steps that directly lead to the goal. "Say your goal is to go to Tahiti a year from now. Mark your calendar and go to a travel agent and get folders on Tahiti. Why don't you also give the agent a non-refundable deposit? At this point, many people will thing 'Are you kidding?' A few will say, 'That's great. If that's what it takes, that's what I'll do.'"

Every popular method of helping to attain your goals involves about the same commitment, work, and effort. Daily review of written-down goals, for instance, is a staple, if only because it means that every day you are again reminded of what your objectives are. It's one thing to think every payday about getting a better job. It's entirely different and more forceful to do it daily.

One method for getting what you want is the formula of speaker and author Zig Ziglar. Participants in his Goals Program fill in details worksheets, which cover benefits from achieving the goal; obstacles to achieving it; knowledge or skills needed to achieve it; individuals who can help in achieving it; and specification of a short-term, immediate action plan.

Once filled in, Ziglar's Goals Sheets are reviewed daily by participants and updated as required. This may seem like tedious work but Ziglar, Grant, and the rest of the goals theorists assure it is well worth it. Says Waitley: "Goals become the action plans and game plans that winners dwell on in intricate detail knowing that achievement is almost automatic when the goal becomes an inner commitment."

SESSION 6
Conflict Management

Objective

The objective of **Session 6** in **PeopleTek's** *Leadership Journey*® is to understand effective conflict management.

This will include the following:

- Become more aware of your own conflict style

- Recognize the conflict styles of others

- Introduce an understanding of effective conflict management and how to use it to your advantage

- Determine if you are over or under using your Conflict Mode Style and determine how that is impacting your leadership skills and abilities

EXERCISE 6.1 – Conflict Style - Prework

Complete your online assessment (Thomas-Kilmann Conflict Instrument) and circle where you feel below.

Competing	High	Med	Low
Collaborating	High	Med	Low
Compromising	High	Med	Low
Avoiding	High	Med	Low
Accommodating	High	Med	Low

1. What approaches do you use the most, according to your assessment:

2. So, how can you use effective conflict management to your advantage? Are there any styles you need to ensure you don't over-use or under-use? If yes, what are they?

Overview of Conflict Modes

★ *Definitions*

1. <u>Conflict</u> is any situation where your concerns or desires differ from another person's
2. <u>Assertiveness</u> is the extent to which an individual attempts to satisfy his own concerns
3. <u>Cooperativeness</u> is the extent to which an individual attempts to satisfy another person's concerns

★ *Cooperativeness/Assertiveness Dimensions*

★ *Your Effectiveness in handling conflict depends on two factors:*

○ Knowing when to use each mode
○ Having the skills to perform each mode well

5 Modes of Conflict Worksheet

Mode:	Competing	Collaborating	Compromising	Avoiding	Accommodating
Two Dimensions	*High assertive, low cooperative*	*High assertive, high cooperative*	*Intermediately assertive and cooperative*	*Low assertive, low cooperative*	*Low assertive, high cooperative*
I win/lose:					
Others win/lose:					
Skills:					
If overused:					
If underused:					
This Mode is Useful When ...					

SESSION 7

The Strategic Action Plan

Objective

Learn a new tool for handling projects or solving problems; *The Strategic Action Plan (SAP).* This tool was previously known as "The Brown Paper Process". This planning and problem solving tool, is designed to take anything from where it is today to where you want or desire it to be. It can be used to solve problems and set plans. While this is a very good tool and process, it is not meant to be a full project planning process.

The Seven Key Steps for the *Strategic Action Plan*

Step 1

Agree on mission/objective for the Strategic Action Plan

Step 2

Agree on a number of focus areas (Streams) that are key for achieving this mission

Step 3

Discuss and agree on the 'TO BE's' for each of these STREAMS

Step 4

Identify the CRITICAL SUCCESS FACTORS (CSF's) to sanity check the Streams – there is a problem if CSF is not covered by a stream

Step 5

Discuss and agree on the 'AS IS' for each of these Streams - an honest and consensus evaluation is needed.

Step 6

Discuss and agree on the HOW TO's for <u>each of the streams</u>

Step 7

Ensure accountability. Assign owners for each stream and for the "HOW TO" steps.

How to Create a Successful Strategic Action Plan

1. Promote and explain The Strategic Action Plan to team members.

2. Appoint a core team (no more that 15 people) to create a straw Strategic Action Plan on key focus areas.

3. Core team presents straw Strategic Action Plan to full team to gain buy-in, alignment, feedback, identify opportunities (yellow post-its) and issues (red post its).

4. Strategic Action Plan is presented to key technology leaders and business partners to gain buy-in, alignment, feedback, identify opportunities (yellow post-its) and issues (red post its).

5. (Optional) Hold *Strategic Action Plan* Fair to present plan and gain staff buy-in and feedback to create final version of plan.

6. Ensure all STREAMS have owners (Accountability) and all "HOW TO's" have owners (Responsibility).

7. Display Strategic Action Plan in visible area. Replace status with printed graphics whenever possible and mark off "How To's" as completed.

Successful Tips for Strategic Action Plan

➢ Ensure everyone understands the process

➢ Start with a simple compelling objective

➢ Focus on the To Be's / Streams and describe the ideal scenario in SMART goal format if possible.

Sample Strategic Action Plan

TO BECOME An A+ SERVICE ORGANIZATION by 12/31/xx

	1	2	3	4	5	6
A	Stream	AS IS	How To			To Be
B	TEAM Owner: Jones	The team is reactive and needs to move to a more proactive role	All teams have monthly 1:1s Owner: DLs	Identify technical skill gaps within team Owner: K. Collins	Implement Knowledge Share program Owner: J. Stable	A highly motivated & technical high performance team by 12/31/xx
C	CUSTOMERS Owner: A. Smith	A lack of understanding of customer needs	Identify Customer needs Owner: M. Day			Customer satisfaction by consistently exceeding expectations by 12/31/xx
D	PROCESS Owner: B. Smith	Few processes mapped & documented	Identify and map processes Owner: K.Smith	Align the process Owner: J. Alan	Automate processes Owner: B. Smith	Streamlined & automated core processes by 12/31/xx
E	METRICS Owner: C.Black	No metrics between us and business partners	Meet business partners to discuss metrics Owner: J. Jones	Align metrics with partners Owner: K. Jones	Plan monthly updates with partners Owner: M. Dyer	Set of metrics that measure effectiveness by 12/31/xx
F	MARKETING Owner: F, Brown	Little or no marketing of services	Create marketing plan Owner: B. Holby			Services and results clearly communicated by 12/31/xx
G	CRITICAL SUCCESS FACTORS	*Reliable Systems / Global Standards / Documented processes / Technical Excellence / Understand Customer Needs*				

SESSION 8
Listening & Communication

Objective

Communication is one of the most important skills there is for understanding effective leadership. Once a vision, mission, goals and measures are created, and even when they are in development, a leader needs to understand the techniques of effective communication.

In **Session 8** of **PeopleTek's** *Leadership Journey®* we will learn how using all of our senses when listening will lead to effective communication and pay off when dealing with our teams and organizations. We will determine what approach for communicating a message is most appropriate and when to use it. We will uncover our unique listening style and the style of others, and what that means when leading our staff.

LISTENING

> **Complete the Learning To Listen Profile to determine your scores for:**

- **Staying Focused**

- **Capturing The Message**

- **Helping The Speaker**

Your results will reflect your scores for "Above Average", "Average" and "Below Average"

EXERCISE 8.1 — Situational Exercise

Step 1: Situational Exercise

Everyone has a communication horror story – your intentions were honorable but somewhere along the way, the line of communication broke down and disaster occurred.

Tell us about one of those experiences by writing down the key aspects of the story. Think about situations that may have involved cross-cultural, electronic, politically correct, or listening components.

Step 2: Situational Exercise

Review again your preferred listening styles. How could using some of the other styles have helped this situation improve?

COMMUNICATION

So whose problem is it if the communication process doesn't work? To answer that question we have to take a look at all the players.

Communication Components

1. First we have **the sender**. Regardless of how you send your message, your past relationship with people will play a large role in their reception of your message. If they do not know you, they will form an impression based on whatever information is available – speech, clothing, grooming, physical appearance, tone of voice.
2. Then there is **the message** itself. Here we are concerned with choice of words, providing background and rationale, being aware of potential resistance or support for the idea, frequency and repetitiveness of the message.
3. Next comes **the communication channel**. Some channels of communication are richer such as face-to-face, while others are leaner, like flyers or brochures. It seems obvious that you would not communicate highly personal and/or controversial information via a memo to the general population, but some managers lack the sense of when to use the appropriate channel. A lot more about this in a moment.
4. Let us not forget the **receiver.** The receiver interprets your message and you have very little control over how that happens. Does the person have 'hot buttons', do they feel strongly about certain values, are they rigid or flexible? If you tie your message to something the person feels strongly about, you can increase the odds that they will listen to you. The reason you have so little control is that the receiver is affected by perception, personality, attitudes, motivation, all things that will color the way the message is received and interpreted.
5. Lastly we have **the feedback loop**. This component allows you to check that the message was received in the way you intended. How you get feedback depends on the medium used. If you are talking face to face, you can see the person's expression (assuming you can read them correctly!). On phone calls, you can always ask the receiver to restate what they heard; however, using emails gives you very little to work with.

EXERCISE 8.2 — Communication

So, let us try to answer this question – whose problem is it if the communication process doesn't work?

Think back to your communication horror story. Which of the above communication components played the key role in derailing the process? A key question to ask yourself is what was your intention? What was the purpose of the communication? What did you want to achieve? This is often not obvious. You have to dig deep to get at your intention.

Channels of Communication

Picking the right channel of communication is a key skill for all leaders. To do this well you have to understand the richness of the channel and the type of message best suited for that channel.

➢ **Face to face**. Why is this the richest? Think about tone of voice, posture, gestures, eye contact, and body position.

➢ **Video Conference.** How does this compare to face-to-face?

➢ **Telephone.** What items do you retain here?

➢ **Computer/email/instant messaging**. All you have here is text, although some people try to use smiling faces or phrases in parenthesis to denote their emotional perspective. At least you can customize it to your audience.

➢ **Texting.** How is texting the same or different compared to email?

➢ **Electronic Blasts/Reports, etc.** This is pretty much one size fits all – everyone on distribution gets the same message.

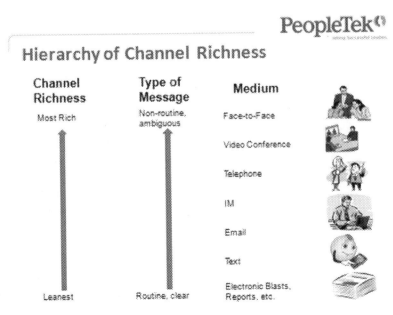

PeopleTek

Hierarchy of Channel Richness

Channel Richness	Type of Message	Medium
Most Rich	Non-routine, ambiguous	Face-to-Face
		Video Conference
		Telephone
		IM
		Email
		Text
Leanest	Routine, clear	Electronic Blasts, Reports, etc.

EXERCISE 8.3 — Leadership Style and Communication

➤ So how does your personality and leadership style impact your message and how you communicate it? Think back to the results of your **Myers–Briggs** and **DiSC** instruments.

➤ How does your style impact the way you send your message, how you formulate the message itself, the medium or channel that you pick, and the way the message is received?

➤ What kinds of things can you do to improve your communication process? Take a few moments and record your thoughts below.

	Things I can do to improve my communication style
Me as sender	
Message itself	
Communication Channel	
Receiver of the message	
Feedback Loop	

Communication Planner

Date:

TOPIC:

Audience:

Reason:

Desired Outcome:

Main Points:

Anticipated questions & responses:

Q:

A:

Q:

A:

Checklist: Will the communication answer the following questions?

1. What is going to happen?   Y   N

2. Why is it going to happen?   Y   N

3. How is it going to happen?   Y   N

4. When is it going to happen?   Y   N

5. Who is it going to impact and how?   Y   N

6. How will concerns be addressed?   Y   N

If response to any of these questions is "No" your communication may not result in the desired outcome. Please consider revising your plan to include any required information.

1-to-1 Worksheet

Name:	Date:	Time:

Progress on Goals/Stats:

Progress on Development Plan:

Status Report Discussion:

Open Discussion: (upward feedback: What do I do that helps you? What can I do better? What negative or positive trends have you recognized in the department? Any process improvement ideas?)

Leader Signature:	Employee Signature:

SESSION 9

Understanding and Managing Change

Objective

In **Session 9** of **PeopleTek's** *Leadership Journey*®, we will **concentrate on** discussing **reality** together. This means taking many of the **concepts, techniques and learnings** from the past weeks and putting them together to actually have the experience of reality in this *Leadership Journey*®. We will be introducing each of the processes that effective leaders do as they are implementing their vision, mission, goals, measures= behavior (**VMGM=B**). These processes include communication, change and conflict.

The first and most important process that comes from implementing your vision or mission is change. You, as well as your team, will experience change and conflict once you begin to carry out your vision. It is imperative that you understand how you are being impacted by change, and also how your team is being impacted. Session 9 will provide the techniques and strategies to effectively understand change and what you as the leader can do to minimize the adverse effects of change and prevent loss of productivity. Remember, the change is not only impacting your staff it is also impacting yourself!!!

Leadership and Change

It doesn't matter whether a change is initially seen as positive or negative; when people's expectations are significantly disrupted the end result is resistance. The way people manifest this resistance differs according to how they view the change.

They either have what is defined as a **Negative Response to Change** or a **Positive Response to Change.** In both "response to change styles", there are distinct stages through which people pass whenever they feel trapped in a change they don't want and can't control. Eight distinct phases are associated with Negative Response to Change and five distinct phases are associated with Positive Response to Change**.**

Negative Response to Change

As you might expect, change that is unexpected and unwanted may be met with significant resistance. Individuals may react in what is defined as a Negative Response to Change. There are **8 Distinct Phases** associated with **Negative Response to Change**.

Phase 1 - Stability. This phase precedes the announcement of the change. It represents the present state.

Phase 2 - Immobilization. This initial reaction is shock. Reactions may vary from temporary confusion to complete disorientation. The impact of change is so alien to the person's frame of reference that he/she is unable to relate to what is happening.

Phase 3 - Denial. The individual is unable to assimilate new information. Change related information is often rejected or ignored. Common reactions are "It won't happen to me" or "If I ignore it, it will go away".

Phase 4 - Anger. This phase is characterized by frustration and hurt, often manifested by indiscriminate lashing out. These emotions are often directed at friends and family, typically the ones most likely to be supportive.

Phase 5 - Bargaining. Here people begin negotiating to avoid the negative impact of change. Examples could be "I'll do it but I need an deadline extension" or "I'd like to be reassigned". This marks the beginning of acceptance.

Phase 6 - Depression. This is represented by feelings of victimization and helplessness, resignation to failure and disengagement from one's work. At this point the full weight of the negative change is finally acknowledged.

Phase 7 - Testing. People regain a sense of control by acknowledging the new limitations but exploring ways to redefine goals.

Phase 8 - Acceptance. Individuals respond to change more realistically, but still may not like it.

Working with team members as they pass through the negative response model is time consuming because providing the appropriate support at each phase consumes time and energy. Nevertheless, the price of a valued team member's not being able to complete the sequence can be even more costly. When someone gets stuck at one or more of the phases, dysfunctional behavior typically escalates and consumes an inordinate amount of time and energy for all concerned.

Positive Response to Change

People may also exhibit resistance to changes that are normally considered positive. Think about getting married, having a baby, or getting a new job. There are **Five Distinct Phases** associated with **Positive Resistance to Change.**

Phase 1 – Uninformed optimism. This is an overly idealistic perception of what is coming. Generally the individual does not have a good picture of what the change will entail. They have a naïve enthusiasm based on insufficient data.

Phase 2 – Informed pessimism. Reality hits! As the change unfolds, we realize that what we expected does not come to pass and much (for which the person is not prepared) begins to take place. Public and/or private checking out may occur.

This represents a withdrawal from the whole change process. Checking out manifests itself either publicly by displaying overt behavior or privately by going underground with your detachment. Public checking out is less destructive since there is an acknowledgement of the problems.

Phase 3 – Hopeful realism. Beginning to see the light at the end of the tunnel. As more concerns are resolved, you become increasingly confident.

Phase 4 – Informed optimism. Individuals realize optimism based on a realization of the true situation. Some successful experience is realized.

Phase 5 – Completion. This is the end to the process of change where new behaviors and attitudes are integrated into the person.

Working with team members exhibiting a Positive Response to Change may seem easier. Keep in mind however, that all change is expensive; you either pay for what you want or you pay for not getting what you want, but there is always a price to pay.

Positive and negative responses to change are adapted from Connor, D. (1993). Managing At The Speed Of Change.

EXERCISE 9.1 — Techniques for Handling Change

Techniques for Handling Change

So, as a leader, what should you do to handle change with your team members? Think of the models presented above. Consider the following questions and record your answers for discussion.

➤ What recent change has happened in your organization or in your personal life?

➤ Where are you in the model and what can you do for yourself?

➤ What should you look for in your team members? Where are they in the model? What can you do to help them?

Techniques

Here we are going to come up with some specific techniques to use with your team to manage change. **Look back** at the **mission/vision/objectives** that **you developed** for **your department**. Is anything different that you are now requiring of your team members – changing vision, different behaviors, new approach to reward and recognition, and specific measurements?

EXERCISE 9.2 – Previous Versus New

Vision/Mission/Objectives

PREVIOUS MISSION/ VISION/OBJECTIVES	NEW MISSION/VISION/OBJECTIVES

EXERCISE 9.2 – Previous Versus New

Vision/Mission/Objectives continued…

Change Exercise 1

How will your team members react to these changes? Think of a previous change that they had to deal with. How did they react? Did they get stuck in a specific phase?

TEAM MEMBER'S NAME	REACTION TO CHANGE

EXERCISE 9.2 – Previous Versus New

Vision/Mission/Objectives continued…

What techniques are appropriate to use with your team members who are in different phases of the negative change model? Another way to look at this is to ask how you are planning on dealing with change? How will you communicate it? What methods will you use?

CHANGE PHASES	TECHNIQUES
Stability	
Immobilization	
Denial	
Anger	
Bargaining	
Depression	
Testing	
Acceptance	

Change Responses & How They Relate to DiSC Styles

How you perceive your environment and your ability to influence it determine which of four **DiSC "Response Styles"** you are using in a situation.

	Have Influence	Lack Influence
Comfortable Environment	**i** Influence	**S** Steadiness
Challenging Environment	**D** Dominance	**C** Conscientiousness

DiSC Response Styles

IN COMFORTABLE ENVIRONMENT	**i's** – feel influential, likely to approach other people, volunteer to lead, ask for help, persuasive and attract attention.
	S's – feel they lack influence, look for ways to be supportive and contribute to shared goals with others. Feel what is good for others will be good for you.
IN CHALLENGING ENVIRONMENT	**D's** - feel influential, initiate action, respond quickly, take certain risks, and get straight to the point
	C's – feel they lack influence, tend to work within an area of personal discretion to ensure your standards are met and personal integrity is maintained.

Managing Change

Strategies for each DiSC style

DOMINANCE

- Create short range goals so that you feel a sense of accomplishment and that the process is moving forward.
- Learn rules, goals and expectations and what you can do to meet them.
- Clarify your accountabilities, know when to initiate action, consult or wait for others.
- Work on your transition plan to get through the change.

iNFLUENCE

1. Identify advantages and opportunities and explore them; get to know new colleagues, clients.
2. Discuss with others new expectations & assess how you and others can get comfortable with them.
3. Gather people for constructive discussion of what change(s) means and how to cope with them to be creative.
4. Think about your goals and how they affect others.

STEADINESS

1. Find out why these changes are necessary from those who initiated the change.
2. Find out what is going to change, when and how it will affect you (and your team).
3. Find a support group to learn what others are doing with this change.
4. Visualize how you will be in the future; hold it in your mind.

CONSCIENTIOUSNESS

1. Learn what is expected of you in the new situation.
2. Determine what new skills or knowledge you may need and how to obtain them.
3. Identify short term objectives, develop temporary ways to get things done, exchange observations and ideas with others.
4. Identify what needs to be done, keep things moving, decide what issues you can do something about versus those that you can't.

EXERCISE 9.3 – Change Exercise

Answer the following questions as you consider a change that is affecting you now.

CHANGE Exercise

- Select a change you are facing (that you are willing to share):

1. Was this change voluntary (self initiated) or involuntary (externally driven)?

2. How did / does this change make you feel?

3. What emotions does it invoke?

4. If your change was voluntary, how do you think your answers would differ if it was involuntary?

EXERCISE 9.3 – Change Case Study

Scenario

The team you have been working with has undergone a complete change in leadership and team members. You and the team members are familiar with the **DiSC** instrument. Your new leader is a blend of Steadiness and Conscientiousness. The members of your team are comprised of the following **DiSC** styles:

Dominance	Influence	Steadiness	Conscientiousness
4	4	2	1

Your position has changed from technical lead programmer to project manager which includes making sure (despite the change in team members and new leadership) that all deliverables are on time and the project completed within budget.

1. How did you accept the transition from leader programmer to project manager?

2. What style would be most appropriate to get you engaged or embrace the change quickly?

3. Who (what style) do you think would be most reluctant to accept the changes?

4. As the project manager, how will you facilitate the team's transition from resistance to acceptance and commitment?

SESSION 10

Team Roles and Magic Dust

Objective

Become familiar with the **6 Types Of Working Genius**

In Session 10 of PeopleTek's *Leadership Journey®*, we look at our unique skills and abilities and how they transcend to our behavior on a team. We will also learn how effective leaders understand that not all roles can be played by everyone. We must utilize others for the skills and abilities they do best.

How do we find out what they are? How do effective leaders use this for motivation? In Session 10 we will look at the importance of being able to identify unique skills and abilities in ourselves and others. By looking at the various roles we play on a team we can determine if we are asking ourselves to be everything to everyone, rather than focusing on what we do best.

Also during this session we will examine what happens when we are placed on a team (or we place ourselves on a team) that doesn't directly tie into our **"Magic Dust"**. How do we feel, what do we think, how do we behave?

EXERCISE 10.1 – The 6 Types Of Working Genius

Think of a time when you used your skills and abilities or your Magic Dust.

- ○ How did you feel?
- ○ What did you do?
- ○ Have you ever asked others to do this?
- ○ How did they feel?

Review what you have learned about yourself from the **6 Types Of Working Genius**:

1. Are you **over-using** any of your **skills and abilities**?

2. Are you **under-using** any of your **skills and abilities**?

3. Did you experience any **"a-ha's"** about your **essence**?

4. Did you experience any **insights** about your staff?

5. Jot down the key points you have learned through this exercise in your **Leadership Travel Journal**.

6. What are your results for the following areas:

   Working Genius   1. _____   2. _____
   Working Competency   1. _____   2. _____
   Working Frustration   1. _____   2. _____
   Does it help you identify your **Magic Dust**?

7. Are there certain positions that would better suit your personal skills and abilities?

SESSION 11

Director/VP Case Study Putting It All Together

Objectives

In **Session 11** of **PeopleTek's** *Leadership Journey*® we will:

➢ Understand how all the materials apply to real life situations in our business world and personal life.

➢ Apply Journey learnings (tools, techniques, behaviors) to reduce conflict and make us more successful.

➢ Have the opportunity to hear the VMGMs for some of the participants and provide them with class feedback

➢ Team Journeys: See also custom information which will be distributed electronically by your Executive Coach/Facilitator

Well at last we finally get to use all the tools and techniques from the **Leadership Journey**® apply them in a real situation. During **Session 11** you will be able to see how decisions are made and how the tools can help us to understand what has happened and some techniques on how to take corrective action.

Tools are effective if you put them to use. As effective leaders you now have techniques that can help you understand yourself and others. The more clarity you have about your vision and mission the better you will be able to carry out all other leadership actions.

Director / VP Case Study

Overview:

A director in an engineering company has worked for the same company and had the same role for seven years. The Director oversees Customer Relations, where the responsibilities include being the liaison between the product development department and the customer. The Director manages a small team of 3, and the customers get along very well with the Director and the small team of three. The Director is knowledgeable, fast paced, and results oriented towards solving customer issues. The Director wants to get promoted and advance in the company to the position of Vice President.

Last month the engineering auditor left the company after numerous audit infractions were discovered. To save money, rather than fill this position, the auditor responsibilities are being split between The Director and the Director's leader, the VP. Due to this change, several problems have arisen between the VP and the Director.

INFORMATION FOR EXERCISES

1. You have been hired as a consultant to review the situation and determine what actions the Director and VP can take to move the business forward and resolve the audit issues.

2. The VP wants The Director to manage the auditors and ensure the infractions are addressed, resolved, and documented. If they are not, the VP feels the Director needs to hold the audit team accountable. The Director does not like doing this and avoids it at all costs. Instead, the Director runs to the thing that is most comfortable for the Director: relationships with customers.

3. The VP believes the Director is not assertive enough. The Director needs to be responsible for getting the audit team together to prepare monthly reports and hold meetings to gain concurrence on who will solve the problems and what actions will be taken. The Director and the team must investigate and gather information from others, organize it, and present back their findings. The VP believes that the Director should "get after people" to obtain the required information.

4. When the Director is asked what he/she thinks about the new responsibilities, the Director says he/she likes them and is making progress. The Director talks about the many activities going on with the customers and doesn't come to staff meetings prepared to discuss the audit issues, documentation, or report/status updates.

5. The VP thinks the Director avoids the discussions with the audit team, seems unconcerned about the work, and is not interested in "owning" these new responsibilities despite being a priority.

6. The Director believes he/she is being criticized unjustly and thinks the VP is being too hard on him/her, too "nit-picky." The Director says that he/she will do what is wanted, but that the VP does not provide the Director with specific details of the desired results. The Director has told the consultant that he/she feels hurt and unappreciated, but acknowledges that he/she would never tell the VP that.

7. The VP feels the Director lacks focus, spends too much time on the phones with the customers, and isn't detail oriented or interested in resolving the audit issues. They are in a fast-paced production environment that has government responsibilities, and must ensure audits are conducted monthly, with the results published in compliance with audit guidelines.

8. The consultant asked both the Director and the VP if they had shared their thoughts and concerns with each other, both responded "no".

9. The VP believes that if the Director performed these operational audit responsibilities well, he/she could be a strong candidate for the next Vice President position.

➤ The Director's instrument results:

MBTI:	INFP
DiSC:	High "I" High "D"
Listening:	Low in Staying Focused
Conflict:	Above the line in:
	Compromising, avoiding, and accommodating
Working Genius (2)	Galvanizing and Wonder

➤ The VP's instrument results:

MBTI:	ESTJ
DiSC:	High "D" High "C"
Listening:	Low in Capturing The Message
Conflict:	Above the line in competing,
	below the line in accommodating and
	avoiding
Working Genius (2)	Tenacity and Enablement

Common challenges in business are working with others, understanding their preferences, and communicating to them in the language they understand and can relate to.

Now that you've gone through the Leadership Journey program, what tools, concepts, processes and techniques could have been used to avoid these situations?

EXERCISE 11.1

Based on the differing styles for the VP and Director, what do <u>you</u> view their issues to be?

EXERCISE 11.2:

Using the tool results, explain the problems between the VP and Director (from <u>their</u> possible point of view) focusing on the following questions:

1. What do they each view the problem(s) to be?

2. What issues may they experience when trying to resolve their conflicts?

3. What do you think they need to consider when working with the other person? How could they better relate to each other?

    •   The Director could consider changing:

    •   The VP could consider changing:

SESSION 12

Wrap-up and Graduation

Objectives

✓ Hear the remainder of the teams VMGMs and provide them with class feedback

✓ Reflect and share learnings on how life will be different as a result of the Journey

✓ Finalize the *Leadership Journey®* **"At a Glance" profile**

✓ Understand the value of networking

✓ Team Journeys: See also custom information which will be distributed electronically by your Executive Coach/Facilitator

✓ Complete the course evaluation

Graduation!

Congratulations! We are finally graduating from **PeopleTek's** *Leadership Journey®*. During graduation you will have the opportunity to reflect on what you have learned thus far in *your Leadership Journey* and make a commitment to continue your leadership development.

You will do this by completing the *Leadership Journey®* **"At a Glance" profile**. This allows you to recap all that you have learned during our time together and plan for future travels. You should keep it close to you so that it can serve as a daily reminder of your thoughts, reflections, aspirations, a–ha's and plans. I wish you well on your future journeys, wherever they may take you!

In addition, in this session we will discuss the importance of having a network. This is one of the most important things a leader can have as a resource. Remember, sometimes it's not what you know but who you know.

PeopleTek's *Leadership Journey®* "At a Glance"

PeopleTek's *Leadership Journey's®* **"At a Glance"** profile allows you to summarize the awareness that you developed for each of the major instruments and/or exercises that you completed during the **Leadership Journey®.**

➢ Complete the AWARENESS column by recording insights, 'a-ha' experiences, new connections or reflections that you experience.

➢ Complete the FUTURE ACTION column by recording what tasks, activities or plans you will undertake in the future to help you realize or implement the treasures you have acquired.

Utilize your *Journey* results as you go along; however, don't hesitate to go back and add/modify insights as thoughts link together. This will serve as a continuing reminder as we complete our work together, and as you continue your personal Journey.

What do you want to get out of this Journey?

Session	Instrument/topic	Awareness	Future Actions
1	**Personal Accountability (QBQ)**	What was your insight?	What behaviors do I need to change to really hold myself accountable as a leader?
2	**Leadership Essence ("Magic Dust")**	What have you identified as your leadership essence? What special skills and abilities have you identified?	How are you going to live it?
3	**Myers Briggs Type Indicator**		
4	**DISC Type**		
5	**Vision/Mission Statements Instrument/topic**		
5	**Strategy/Goals/ Measures of Success**	What is your Strategic Focus (operational excellence, product innovative, or customer intimate?)	

6	**Preferred Conflict Approach**		
7	**Strategic Action Plan**	Is there a current opportunity for you to apply this instrument to solve a problem or drive improvement?	
8	**Learning To Listen Tool**		
9	**Change Management**		
10	**6 Types Of Genius Tool**		
11	**Putting it All Together**	eg. Is there a current situation where you can apply these learnings?	
All	**Personal Networking**		
All	**What is the one thing you have been doing that you want to leave behind?**		
All	**What is the one new thing you will take continuing on your Leadership Journey?**		

Self Discovery:

RATE YOUR EFFECTIVENESS IN EACH OF THE SKILLS BELOW

1=poor 10=superb

Awareness of skills and behaviors (of self) _____

Awareness of skills and behaviors (of others) _____

Magic Dust (knowing and leveraging your strengths) _____

Vision/Mission/Goals (ALL of your behaviors) support them) _____

Communication (your message is accurately interpreted) _____

Clarity of roles, responsibilities, and desired results _____

Accountability (for self) _____

Managing and Addressing CONFLICT _____

Influence (how you present yourself to others) _____

continued

RATE YOUR EFFECTIVENESS IN EACH OF THE SKILLS BELOW

1=poor 10=superb

RELATIONSHIPS (building and maintaining) ———

FEEDBACK (both giving and receiving) ———

Inspiration (empowering and stretching others) ———

Continual Learning (embracing and leading through change) ———

IDENTIFY YOUR STRENGTHS, TARGET DEVELOPMENT AREAS, IDENTIFY WHO CAN HELP, AND TAKE ACTION!

Existing Strengths (scores 8 – 10):

Areas to develop:

Who can help?

Next steps and "by when":

Journey at a Glance – VMGM=B pg 1

Vision, Mission, Goals, Measures = Behaviors (Your Name)

Vision	
Mission	

Goal	Action	Target Date	Success Measures
Goal 1:			
Goal 2:			
Goal 3:			

Leadership Behaviors	Steps I'll Take	Target Date	Success Indicators
Goal 1:			
Goal 2:			
Goal 3:			

Note: Include how you will use your *Magic Dust* (or at least one strength) even more, and list one or two behaviors you will adjust to reach your VMGM. Get specific; what steps will you take?

Testimonials

When you take the Journey, you obtain feedback regarding your strengths and the differences in the scales which describe your behaviors. You then realize what fits and what doesn't and why you have to approach each person differently once you recognize their differences. —Dr. Abe Fischler

This has been time and money well spent on my team. This is coming back in payoffs multiple times to me. I have noticed positive changes in how my team interacts, and there is more open dialog and trust. We are truly able to do more and with better quality than before. I also have much stronger peer relationships resulting in collaboration and success with our teams. -S. Bhojwani

The training was fantastic! I'd recommend it to anyone who wants to become a better leader, team player or human being!—C. Breinholt

This training guided through a series of self discoveries that hold the secret of improving my effective leadership behavior, techniques and processes. I learnt tools that can connect them to the work I am doing today. -L. Mahate

PeopleTek's Leadership Journey is a very beneficial program for anyone who is in a company environment to help both employees and management teams have considerably more effective interactions and communication. More importantly is that it teaches you how to capitalize on each individual's strength (as well as understand the differences) to better increase the productivity of the group on the whole.

—M. Baker

I enjoyed the Leadership Journey and learning more about my leadership style. More importantly I have learned much about other styles which is very helpful in understanding how and when to proceed with initiative. Change management was also a great tool for me as in today's economic environment there is much change across the board but especially in sales. Having the tools to help the team adjust to change has already been of benefit. I would highly recommend this class to every leader out there and because I believe everyone is a leader...everyone would benefit.

— K. Jones

This Leadership Journey was the best I have been a part of for helping me to gain some perspective on the point of view of others, particularly when you consider their "type." Good instruction!—B. Stanton

All management should take the class. It would facilitate focusing on listening and learning skills. The Journey opens minds to future capacity/growth and assists with how to manage and be managed.—D. Duffy